A Dog's Breakfast

A Dog's Breakfast

A Chef's Guide to Healthy Home Cooking for Your Favorite Pooch

Jess Young

GREAT PLAINS
PUBLICATIONS

Great Plains Publications
345-955 Portage Avenue
Winnipeg, MB R3G 0P9
www.greatplains.mb.ca

Great Plains Publications gratefully acknowledges the financial support provided for its publishing
program by the Government of Canada through the Canada Book Fund; the Canada Council for
the Arts; the Province of Manitoba through the Book Publishing Tax Credit and the Book Publisher
Marketing Assistance Program; and the Manitoba Arts Council.

Design & Typography by Relish Design Studio Inc.
Printed in Canada by Friesens

Library and Archives Canada Cataloguing in Publication

Young, Jess, 1982-
        A dog's breakfast : a chef's guide to healthy home
cooking for your favorite pooch / Jess Young.

ISBN 978-1-926531-07-6

        1. Dogs--Food--Recipes. I. Title.

SF427.4.Y69 2010   636.7'085   C2010-904542-4

To my mom and dad and Jarod, for their love and support

CONTENTS

• Jess with
Charlie
& Peanut

I never used to be a dog person. I never really understood all the fuss about "man's best friend." In fact, I had a feline companion all my childhood and through my early twenties. My attitude changed when I came across an ad in the paper for wiener dogs – aka, the Dachshund. I was intrigued because my mother had had them growing up and I always loved their stubby little legs. So I made an hour-long drive to check out these wiener dogs, and to my surprise, I was smitten. I choose a miniature Dachshund and named him Peanut, my heart, my pal, my dog. Over the years, he's provided me with laughs, love, and the motivation to find the best possible ways to provide a healthy everyday life for him.

I have been in the restaurant trade for twelve years and am committed to providing health-conscious food, but I was having trouble finding nutritious options for my dog. The problem was that most of the dog food I looked at didn't meet his breed's dietary requirements, and in fact was full of fillers that had no benefit except for creating more poop. I started looking for some alterative that would satisfy me. Then it occurred to me: Hey, I'm a chef, why don't I just cook for my Peanut? This decision was made more than four years ago, and I have been providing my little guy (and his new Dachshund buddy that has joined our family) with a more natural diet ever since.

First and foremost, I am neither a veterinarian nor a canine nutritionist. I am a chef. I have been cooking professionally for years in Canada and briefly in Australia. Food is something I am passionate about. In our modern, fast-paced world, food and nutrition are often undervalued. So when you are next impatiently waiting for your lunch with a friend or business client, just remember that there are dedicated people in the kitchen trying to make your dining experience memorable. As a chef and dog lover, I would take it a step further. What about our beloved pets? Don't they deserve the same memorable experience?

When my dogs hear me open that freezer bag of lamb and rice and when they hear the clinking of the spoon I'm using to mix it with their dry food, they know exactly what's up. Providing a memorable food service for them, just as for my human community, is really what delights me. There are many recipes and food ideas out there in books and on the internet, but sadly there is a lot of contradictory information. Should dogs eat

grains? Is garlic okay? This book, and this collection of recipes, is intended to be a safe and simple introduction to the world of dog nutrition.

When I first began gathering information and ideas four years ago, I had no clue that this is where they would end up. I now have two miniature Dachshunds and they are my boys. I'm sure I treat them a little too much like children, but I knew I wanted to research proper nutritional needs for them. So I read a lot of books, visited a lot of websites and talked to various vets. The more I saw my friends' dogs lapping up beer and chewing on the wrong kind of bones, the more I realized there was a general lack of awareness out there about animal diets. Knowing what foods are toxic to your dog is essential. Also, various breeds of dogs generally have different nutritional requirements. So

buying that giant bag of kibble that's always on sale isn't necessarily the best way to provide our dogs with the nutrition they need.

I've assembled a number of recipes here for truly healthy and inventive dog treats, dinners, and even desserts. You don't need to be a chef like me to manage these basic, trouble-free recipes. Most of the ingredients I've used are readily available and you almost certainly have them in your kitchen already.

This book also includes basic information about dogs' dietary needs and what foods they may ingest that are harmful to them (yes, I mean booze). I won't promise that a beer-less diet will mean your puppy lives forever, but nutritious and inventive food for both of you will ensure you enjoy a long and happy relationship together.

• Scout, companion to
Gregg and Ingeborg

Chapter 1

Why cook for your dog?

• **Rufus, companion to Sadie and Declan**

We live in a fast food world where nutrition is often an afterthought. Ease and convenience are usually the chief considerations in how many of us decide what to eat. Our canine companions live in this world with us. The days when our dogs survived on table scraps are long gone. Now, most of us in industrialized countries feed our pooches dry, brown kernels of kibble from easy and convenient bags.

Many of us choose to believe that the companies that make those easy and convenient bags of feed have the best interests of our dogs at heart. You could say the marketing is working. The truth is commercial dog food is often produced with fillers and preservatives and jam-packed with sodium – much like the processed food we see all around us. And it is not the best source of good nutrition. The melamine contamination of wheat gluten from China in 2007 showed this food might even be dangerous. Hundreds, possibly thousands, of dogs in North America died from eating the many brands that used this toxic Chinese ingredient.

The low-down on the ingredients list and the process of the actual making of dog chow is not something we often think about. We may like to believe that kibble includes lots of fresh meat. In fact, the lean cuts of meat from animals taken to the slaughterhouse end up on your family's dinner table. The making of dog chow has much more to do with the rendering plant than the slaughterhouse. After the good cuts of meat have been made into our sirloins and roasts, there are leftover bits and pieces, along with carcasses. These bits and pieces – which include intestines, ligaments, lungs, beaks, teeth, and feet – then make their way to the rendering plant.

This marvel of a mess is then put into a massive vat along with dead zoo animals, road kill, and euthanized dogs and cats from veterinarians. Everything is shredded and then cooked at a temperature of 220°F to 270°F for about an hour. After it goes through the cooling process, a layer of fat forms at the top which is known as "animal fat." The remaining shredded and cooked bits are pressed and dried into various kibbles. This of course is the well-known "meat and bone meal" and "animal by-products" from the ingredients list.

You may wonder why dogs are so eager to gobble up this garbage. It's merely a trickery of their senses. There are chemicals, colouring agents, flavour agents, lubricants, and texturizers that are also put into the kibble. All of these various things are very enticing to a dog. It's like going without lunch and someone putting your favorite greasy food in front of you. Of course you're going to eat it.

Don't get me wrong – not all dog food companies are responsible for this junk. Some actually do have your dog's health in mind. Some pet food companies make excellent food with high-quality ingredients that provide good nutrition for dogs. There are a lot of choices out there. So for the optimum results for your dog's diet, it is best to make a visit to your vet to assess what is most appropriate. I would, however, generally recommend that you give your dog the highest quality pet food and treats you can afford, with the most natural ingredients – preferably made out of fresh meats and natural oils, with small amounts of whole grains, fruits, and vegetables.

I use a brand of commercial dry dog food myself, though I do mix it with home cooking. Because my life is so busy, I usually make a big batch of one of the recipes in this book and then

• Josh, companion to Maike,
Klaus-Peter, Theresa and Christian

• Cooper, companion to Geoff and Andrea

Photo: Emma Braun

Many of us feed our dogs leftovers from the table along with treats. Table scraps and treats should add up to no more than 10 percent of your dog's diet. Fat trim on meats and bones should not be fed to your dog, as it may raise their fat intake too much from their regular day-to-day diet. Cooked fat is known to be carcinogenic to dogs in high quantities.

freeze meal-sized portions. When you cook at home, you control the ingredients. You control the quality and you make something with your own hands and with love in your heart. If we are not comfortable putting additives, random agents, and excessive preservatives into our own bodies, perhaps we should start thinking about our beloved dogs in the same way.

Our dogs' health is ever fluctuating, much as our own. Changes in our environment and lifestyles are challenging our health every minute. There are more allergy and obesity problems appearing in our society every day. This is the same for our dogs, so in addition to regular checkups, it is important to pay close attention to their vitality and diet.

Home cooking seems to be the logical way to give our dogs the nutrition they need. And it is simpler than you might think. The recipes in this book rely on basic ingredients than even the cooking-averse might have in their pantries. I've had a little fun with these offerings, moving from very basic to a bit more extravagant but the techniques and equipment needed to bake up, say, a batch of dog cookies, are plain and simple. In fact, many of the recipes are so basic they can easily involve young children – a great way for the entire family to learn about canine health.

Although you might not like the taste as much as your dog does, every recipe in this book is safe for people too. There are, however, as you will see in the next chapter, some foods and drinks that we may enjoy that your dog really shouldn't have.

Nutmeg, companion to
Jill, Jim and Andrew

Chapter 2
Do's and Don'ts

Miko, companion to Glenn and Russ

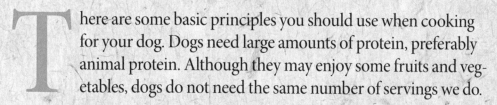

There are some basic principles you should use when cooking for your dog. Dogs need large amounts of protein, preferably animal protein. Although they may enjoy some fruits and vegetables, dogs do not need the same number of servings we do.

Cheap grains are the backbone of commercial kibble. Dogs don't require a lot of grains. There is a debate in the canine nutrition community about whether wheat should be a part of a dog's diet at all.

I choose to use whole-wheat flour whenever possible, or other whole grains like brown rice.

My rules for feeding my dogs are basically the same as what I follow for myself. I try to use healthy products, a lot of rice flour (I have a gluten intolerance), soybeans, fresh meats and vegetables. In my line of work, I have access to scraps of meats. I understand that most of you will not have this luxury. Your best bet is to visit your local butcher and ask what kind of scraps they might have. Usually butchers have tenderloin trim, lamb trim; some may even have salmon or other fish scraps.

Pudgy Pooch?

Instead of whole-milk dairy products, use low-fat yogurt and cheese. Feed your dog leaner meats like chicken and beef as opposed to fattier meats like lamb and pork.

I like to make big batches of food and portion it into small plastic sandwich bags and freeze them. I will pull one portion out at night for the morning, and in the morning mix half of the bag with half dry food.

If you choose to use dry food, it's really important to look at the ingredients list on the package and choose one that has a sufficient amount of meat product in it and not too much filler. Dogs do not need as much fibre as we do so keeping their meals high in protein is very good. I also try as much as I can not to use refined products like table salt, bleached flour, and granulated sugar.

It's important to cook all your meats, poultry, seafood, and eggs thoroughly. Be sure to wash all your produce just as you would your own. Your dog may be partial to certain foods, but try not to eliminate any food groups. Keeping foods simple and fresh will benefit you and your dog. If you find yourself too busy to keep up with a healthy fresh diet, meal planning and making larger batches and freezing is a suitable substitute. Cooking at home with and for your dogs heightens your personal relationship with them. It always delights me to see my dogs' excitement at meal times. My two guys will only finish all their food if it includes some good home cooking.

Don't overfeed your dog!

Overfeeding is one of the main causes of diarrhea, digestive upset, and obesity.

Dogs need meals that are two to three percent of their bodyweight daily. Toy breeds might need slightly more and may need three small meals instead of two.

100 pound dog:	2-3 lbs daily or two meals of 1-1.5 lbs each
75 pound dog:	1.5-2 lbs daily or two meals of 12-18 oz each
50 pound dog:	1-1.5 lbs daily or two meals of 8-12 oz each
25 pound dog:	8-12oz daily or two meals of 4-6 oz each

A Dog's Breakfast

Do

So what can you feed your dog? There are many meats, fruits and vegetables that you and your dog can enjoy together. Here are a few foods that are safe for your pooch.

Offer:

Green beans
Carrots
Cabbage
Pumpkin
Sweet potatoes
Yogurt
Apples
Oatmeal
Grains such as brown rice
Flax seed
Salmon
Lean cuts of meat
Zucchini

Don't

Offer: ALCOHOL

Whether it's a bit of beer at a party or your dog's curiosity just gets the better of him, most of us have fed our dog alcohol at some point or another. I know my dog, Peanut, likes to lick everything, including spills, so I try to be careful.

Alcohol depresses brain function in dogs, much like in people, except your dog will not require a lampshade to dance around with. It is also possible for the consumption of alcohol to send them into a coma, and may even cause their blood to turn acidic. Dogs don't have the proper enzymes to process alcohol and since most dogs are smaller than we are they are more highly sensitive to it. It doesn't take much consumption to cause serious problems.

GRAPES & RAISINS

Although bite-sized and seemingly harmless, grapes and raisins can be dangerous for dogs. Toxicologists have found that canine consumption of these tasty treats can lead to acute kidney failure. The suspected cause of this is a compound that is soluble in water and is indigestible to dogs. It is believed that as few as ten grapes can cause damage.

Yogurt is an excellent source of protein, easily digestible, and a great source of calcium. It is also full of beneficial bacteria that help your dog's digestive and immune systems, especially if your dog has been on antibiotics, which can strip the beneficial bacteria away.

ONIONS & GARLIC

Onions and garlic are poisonous to dogs but unfortunately are included as ingredients in a wide variety of recipes for your pet all over the internet. It's important to avoid these in any form, including powdered.

The consumption of onions or garlic can break down red blood cells over time. It can also lead to anaemia and possible kidney failure due to leaking haemoglobin as dogs simply do not have the enzymes to break down the compound thiosulfate that is found in low levels in both onions and garlic. Thiosulfate is used in the bleaching process and to set dyes. It can remain in the blood stream for up to twenty hours. If a dog eats .5 percent of its body weight in either onion or garlic it can show signs of poisoning. Even as little as five grams per day can mean an unpleasant trip to the vet.

Many puppies are sensitive to texture and temperature. Food at room temperature will be best received.

YEASTY RAW DOUGH

Similar to alcohol, the ingestion of raw dough can cause fatal damage because of the active yeast inside it. In raw bread dough, alcohol is released as the yeast grows. A warm moist environment – like a dog's stomach – is perfect for yeast to grow. Growing yeast in a dog's tummy can prevent blood flow and can lead to blockages causing a protruding abdomen.

Good nuts for your dog:
Peanuts
Almonds
Cashews

Bad nuts:
Macadamia nuts (associated with
    producing muscle tremors
    and even partial paralysis)

CHOCOLATE

Personally I think chocolate has been one of the most controversial substances to feed your dog. Many pet owners claim that it's perfectly acceptable but so many say otherwise. Chocolate contains chemicals called theobromine and methylxanthine. The combination of these chemicals is very dangerous to a dog's system as dogs are incapable of metabolizing and excreting these chemicals as humans can. If your dog has consumed chocolate in any form including cocoa, it can induce vomiting, diarrhea, seizures, rapid breathing, and even coma.

Bones can be a great distraction for your dog or a chance for your dog to clean his teeth. Be careful, however, to offer only sturdy bones that won't splinter – like beef shank bones. No chicken bones, please.

CAFFEINE

Caffeine causes some of the same problems as chocolate, since they share some of the same chemical properties. Caffeine in any form such as coffee, soda pop or tea, produces an accelerated and irregular heart rate. In severe cases it can lead to seizures and a serious upset stomach.

Simple tips for picky eaters

- Don't hover anxiously! Set the food down and walk away nonchalantly. No takers? Remove the food and try again at the next meal.
- Keep it regular! Your dog will learn to anticipate meals and be hungry at that time if you stick to the same feeding schedule.
- Be a happy chef! Teach your dog that dinnertime is exciting by being happy while preparing the meal. Stay calm and positive to avoid anxiety surrounding eating.
- Exercise! Regular exercise will help promote appetite.

A Dog's Breakfast

A few others:

- Citrus oils and extracts may induce vomiting.

- Large amounts of cooked liver can lead to vitamin A toxicity, which affects muscle and bone tissue.

- Mushrooms in large quantities can cause shock.

- Candy, chewing gum or anything with artificial sweeteners can cause lethargy and weakness.

- Anything with a sweet smell can attract your dog, including ibuprofen and antifreeze, which can lead to a serious decrease in blood flow to the kidneys.

- Bones, like chicken bones, fish bones, and T-bones, can splinter and get lodged in their throats.

- Be wary of fruits with pits.

- Avocados contain persin that can cause diarrhea, vomitting and an upset stomach.

Chapter 3
Breeds and Their Diets

A Dog's Breakfast

It has been suggested that specific dog breeds have their own individual dietary needs, much the same as people eating for their blood types. Amazing health results can happen when the breed's diet matches the food commonly eaten where the breed originated. It's still important to consult your vet before introducing any new diets as some dogs may need something specific depending on age or lifestyle.

Certain breeds that are regularly active will have important needs in their diet. Paying attention to these requirements will result in a healthy dog. An improper diet and lack of exercise can lead to obesity and health problems.

Not all dogs come with a pedigree. Mutts should be fed according to the breeds they most resemble. And if there are any concerns, consult your veterinarian.

Try Slammin'
Salmon Cakes, page 77

THE NORTHERNERS

American Eskimo, Siberian Husky, Malamute, and Samoyed

Since these breeds originated up north, their primary diet would have been whales, seals, and some caribou. These types of dogs do very well with high-fat fish. As far as vegetables go, root vegetables are preferred; sweet potatoes provide for a healthy starch. During the North's short growing season, some berries are available, but there are very few grains. As a result these breeds often don't do well on dry dog foods as they contain too many grains.

Try Lord of the Lambs, page 73

THE EUROPEANS

Great Dane, German Shepherd, Dachshund, Rottweiler, Airedale, Old English Sheepdog, Boxer, and Staffordshire Terrier

These breeds thrive the best with red meat proteins such as lamb and beef. Steamed vegetables such as hearty cabbage and kale are very good sources of vitamins. Also including grains such as oats and whole barley will be a benefit. Some of these breeds have a shorter colon and providing the right diet will help avoid intestinal gas problems.

- Abby, companion to Lisa, Andrew, Luke, Kristen, and Robin

Try Quick Tuna
Protein Boost, page 85

THE COASTALS

Labrador Retriever, Spaniels, Newfoundland, and Standard Poodle

These breeds do best with a diet consisting of such protein as goose, duck and fish such as trout. Barley and oats are also a good source of fiber for these dogs. Most water and bird-retrieving breeds need the oils in the fish and duck to aid in healthy joints. Most of their vegetable intake should consist of green beans, potatoes, especially sweet potatoes. And as they say – an apple a day.

A Dog's Breakfast

Try Chicken Rice
Croquettes, page 79

THE HOUNDS

Afghan, Greyhound, Whippet, and Irish Wolfhound

Most hounds, with the exception of Basset hounds and foxhounds, are best with such things as rabbit, turkey, squab, and venison, similar to the prey they originally ate. Barley, potatoes, bulgur, and brown rice included in with their protein diet is beneficial. Apples are also a great vitamin source for these breeds.

Try Potato
Casserole, page 81

THE HUNTERS

Beagle, Foxhound, Irish Setter, Scottish Terrier, Cocker Spaniel, and Basset Hound

These dogs will often do best with a protein of lamb and chicken, and vegetables such as carrots and green beans. Rabbit is good for these breeds. Sweet potatoes and whole barley and oats are a good source of fiber. Also, parsley is a good vitamin source.

Try Lord of
the Lambs, page 73

THE ENGLISH

Border Collie, Toy Poodle, Corgi, Welsh Terrier, and Sheltie

These breeds will flourish with a lamb or chicken protein diet, supplemented with vegetables like carrots and green beans. Sweet potatoes and whole barley and oats are a good source of fiber.

Chapter 4

Appetizers
(biscuits and treats)

Whether it's because we're leaving for the day, rewarding them for a job well done, or just because they're so darn cute, we all give our dogs treats or biscuits, usually on a daily basis.

It's a fact that dogs are highly motivated by food. In turn, we end up often overfeeding with treats, leading to weight gain. A popular reward has been leftover bones or a rawhide, which are both very difficult to digest. Having a healthy alternative can be very beneficial.

Breath Crusher Biscuits

I don't know about your dogs, but mine like to lick the floor regardless of its cleanliness. This really doesn't aid in their already stinky breath, so I like to feed them a couple of these a few mornings a week.

Ingredients

Whole wheat flour	1½ cups
All purpose flour	1 cup
Baking powder	1 tsp
Mint leaves (loosely packed)	½ cup
Milk	¼ cup
Butter or margarine (chilled)	4 tbsp
Whole egg	1
Maple syrup or corn syrup	1½ tbsp

Method

Combine all dry ingredients together and set aside. Finely chop up mint and combine with dry ingredients. Dice chilled butter or margarine and cut into the flour mixture until small pea-sized bits of fat are left. Combine milk, egg, and syrup and mix in with dry ingredients until just combined. Roll out on a floured surface, cut into desired shapes (for medium cookies 2-inch squares). Bake on a baking sheet lined with parchment paper for 20 minutes at 375°F or until golden brown. Cool and store in an airtight container until ready to use. Yields approximately 30 medium biscuits.

Breath Crusher Biscuits variation:
Parsley is a great addition to your dog's diet. It's loaded with vitamins A, B, C and K as well as calcium, potassium, iron, magnesium, phosphorous and even protein! Parsley's chlorophyll will work its magic on foul breath.

Sweetest Desires

Most commercial dog biscuits are savory. This is a way of giving your dog a sweet cookie, without refined white sugar.

Ingredients

Margarine	½ cup
Corn syrup or honey	3 tbsp
Eggs	4
Vanilla	1 tsp
Whole wheat flour	1 cup
Carob powder	¼ cup
Baking powder	½ tsp

Method

Cream margarine and syrup together until pale and fluffy. Add egg and vanilla in one addition. Add dry ingredients and mix until incorporated. For these treats, I like to roll them into little balls in my palm. Bake on a lined sheet for 20 minutes at 350°F. Yields approximately 15 biscuits.

• Lebowski, companion to
  Jeanette and Dale

Born for Corn

Zucchini is one of those vegetables I like because it provides a lot of moisture and my dogs don't even know they're getting their vegetables.

Ingredients

Corn flour	2 cup
Rice flour	1 cup
Whole wheat flour	2 cup
Low sodium chicken broth	2½ cups
Grated zucchini	½ cup

Method

Combine all flours, add zucchini, add chicken broth and form into a dough. I like to form it into a long 2-inch-wide log, and slice ¼ inch slices. Bake on a lined cookie sheet for 20 minutes at 375°F. This recipe yields approximately 40-50 biscuits.

Cheddar and Bacon Bites

Ah, cheddar and bacon, who doesn't like that? I'm sure if this was all I fed my guys they would be pleased. As these are fairly rich I try not to overdo it, even if I get the sad puppy eyes.

Ingredients

Wheat flour	2 cups
Cheddar cheese (grated)	1 cup
Lean bacon (diced, cooked and cooled)	½ cup
Margarine	2 tbsp
Sour cream	1½ cups

Method

Mix flour, cheddar, cooled bacon. Stir in margarine and sour cream until a stiff dough forms. Roll out to ¼ inch thickness. Cut into desired sizes. Bake on a lined cookie sheet for 15-20 min at 350°F. Cool in the oven after you have turned it off and leave the door open a crack. They should be firm to the touch. Makes 6 dozen medium cookies.

Bella, companion to
Rande and Shelley

Perfect pb's

My guys are intrigued any time I give them something with peanut in it. These biscuits give off a nice toasty peanut aroma.

Ingredients

All purpose flour	1 cup
Whole wheat flour	1 cup
Peanuts (chopped)	½ cup
Peanut butter	2 tbsp
Apple (grated)	½ cup
Molasses	2 tbsp
Eggs	2
Yogurt (plain)	4 tbsp

Method

Combine all of the dry ingredients and peanuts and set aside. Combine peanut butter, apple, and molasses. Add to the dry ingredients and mix well. Lastly combine eggs and yogurt and add to dough. Knead dough for a few minutes and roll out to ½ inch thickness and cut into desired shapes (for medium cookies 2-inch squares). Bake on a lined cookie sheet for 20-30 minutes at 350°F or until browned and firm. Makes about 2 dozen small to medium cookies.

A Dog's Breakfast

Cinna Carrot

This is a great way to get vegetables into those veggie-averse dogs (like my own).

Ingredients

Whole wheat flour	2 cups
Cornmeal	¼ cup
Ground cinnamon	½ tsp
Carrot (grated)	¾ cup
Sour cream	½ cup
Vegetable oil	1 tbsp
Honey	1 tbsp
Egg	1

Method

In a large bowl combine dry ingredients. Set aside. In a separate bowl combine carrot, sour cream, oil, honey and egg. Mix with the dry ingredients to form a dough. Roll out on floured surface to ¼ inch thickness, cut into desired shapes. Bake on a lined baking sheet for 15-20 min at 350°F, then let cool completely. Reduce oven to 250°F and bake cookies for another 15-20 minutes until hard.

Mini carrots are a great dog snack. Crunchy and sweet, they're high in fibre and potassium and are an exceptional source of vitamin A and C. That makes them a snack that benefits your dog's eyes, immune system, and digestive system!

Chapter 5
Entrées

There is nothing a dog loves more than his main meal. And he will doubly appreciate it if it is home cooked. If, like me, you are run ragged by life, try supplementing commercial dry food with one of the recipes that follow. "Lord of the Lambs" on the following page is usually on the menu at our house.

Lord of the Lambs

This recipe is something I feed my dogs every day. Before I started feeding them Lord of the Lambs, their food dish would sit with food in it all day. Now it's emptied immediately, except for some picked out vegetables. They're sneaky like that.

I pull out a bag each day from the freezer and divide it up between two meals. I use about a cup of lord of lamb mixed with a cup of dry commercial kibbles.

Ingredients

Lamb (diced)	1 lb
Lean bacon (diced)	½ lb
Zucchini (small dice)	1 cup
Carrots (small dice)	1 cup
Brown rice or barley	3 cups (cooked)

Note: *Since I work in a restaurant I use our lamb scraps, but going to your local butcher and asking for diced lamb will work as well. Or substitute with another protein source.*

Method

First cook the rice or barley, following the product's cooking instructions. Set aside. Place a deep saucepan on medium heat. When pan is hot add bacon, cook down until it starts to release some fat. Add your diced lamb. Cook until browned. Add vegetables, cook until soft. Finally add your cooked rice or barley and toss just to incorporate everything. I feed this to my dogs every day because it's healthy and super easy. Portion into smaller bags of about 1½ cups and keep in freezer.

• Poppy and Folly,
companions
to Margaret and
David

Photo: Emma Brown

Meat à la Loaf

*Don't be afraid to add more vegetables or play around with them
to figure out what your dog prefers.*

Ingredients

Barley	½ cup
Low sodium chicken broth	4 cups
Lean ground beef	1½ lbs
Sour cream	½ cup
Whole eggs	2
Rolled oats	½ cup
Green cabbage (finely sliced)	¼ cup
Zucchini (finely diced)	¼ cup
Spinach (finely sliced)	¼ cup
Vegetable oil	1 tbsp

Method

Combine barley and broth in heavy-bottomed pot,
bring to a boil. Reduce the heat to a simmer, cook
until soft to the bite, about 30-40 minutes, and set
aside. Combine other ingredients and add to barley
mixture. Mix thoroughly. Put into a lightly oiled loaf
pan and bake at 350°F for approximately an hour
or until it reaches 160°F on a cooking thermometer.
Will make enough for about four meals.

Slammin' Salmon Cakes

I like this recipe a lot mostly because dogs don't have much fish in their dry food, and the salmon provides a lot of good omega fats.

Ingredients

Salmon fillet (pin bones removed)	10 oz
Egg	2
Cornmeal	3 tbsp
Sweet potato (diced small)	1 med sized
Carrot	1 med sized
Green beans (diced)	1 cup
Celery (diced)	1 stalk
Yogurt	½ cup
Fresh dill	1 tbsp finely chopped
Oil (for browning)	1 tbsp

Method

Cook salmon in a 375°F oven until it reaches 130°F. Cool salmon down. Combine the salmon, egg, cornmeal and mix well. Form this mixture into patties. Dust the formed patties with a little more cornmeal, and brown in a lightly oiled pan until golden brown and set aside. Sauté the potato and carrot until just soft, not mushy, add other vegetables and continue cooking until soft. Cut up salmon cakes into chunky pieces and mix with the cooked vegetables. Mix yogurt and dill and stir into your mix. Makes about 3-4 meals.

The Omega-3 fatty acids found in fish that are so good for you are also good for your dog. Omega-3-rich foods support the optimal functioning of the heart, eyes, immune and skeletal system, skin, and coat.

• Claudia, companion
to Debbie and Stephen

Chicken Rice Croquettes

These are very convenient. I freeze them and offer them to my dogs as treats.

Ingredient

Skinless boneless chicken thighs (cooked)	2 lbs
Cooked brown rice	½ cup
Carrot (diced)	¼ cup
Spinach (finely sliced)	1 cup
Yogurt (plain)	1 tbsp
Egg	1
Bread crumbs	½ cup

Method

Finely mince chicken, or put in a food processor. Set aside. Cook carrots until soft and mix with spinach, yogurt, egg, and rice. Mix well. Add bread crumbs and mix. If the mix is too moist add a little more bread crumbs. Form mixture into bite-sized patties and dredge in a little flour. Place a pan on medium heat and place a tbsp of vegetable oil in hot pan and lightly brown on each side. Cool down slightly and serve to your dog. Makes about 25.

Potato Casserole

Sweet potato is nutritious. This is a delicious way to get vital nutrients into your dog.

Ingredients

Sweet potato (boiled and sliced)	3 cups
Green beans (small diced)	¼ cup
Carrot (grated)	¼ cup
Cottage cheese	½ cup
Whole milk	¼ cup
Cheddar cheese (grated)	¼ cup

Method

Toss together the green beans, carrot, and cottage cheese. Cover the bottom of a lightly greased casserole dish with some of the sweet potato. Add a layer of vegetable mixture. Continue to alternate vegetable and potato layers, ending with sliced potato. Then pour the whole milk evenly over entire thing. Finish with sprinkling the cheese on top. Bake for 15-20 minutes at 375°F or until the cheese is melted and browned. Cool down and serve. Makes about 4 meals.

Note: If your dogs require a lot of protein in their diet just add a cup of cooked lean ground beef or lamb to the vegetables and cottage cheese mixture.

• Patch, companion
to Pamela, Bill,
Samantha and Sage

Quick-time Quiche

Personally, I like to make this into small tarts that I can just pull out of the fridge for a quick snack. At first my guys were a little wary of the texture, but once they discovered the tuna and cheese they were sold.

Ingredients

Eggs	4
Heavy cream	3 tbsp
Light flaked tuna	3 tbsp
Cheddar cheese (grated)	3 tbsp
Fresh parsley (finely chopped)	2 tsp
20 cm pie shell or a dozen mini non-sweet tart shells	

Method

Whisk together egg and heavy cream. Add remaining ingredients.

Bake empty shells until lightly golden according to instructions on the package. Pour entire contents into pie shell, or if using tart shells equally divide mixture up between them. For larger quiche bake for 15-20 minutes at 350°F or until filling is no longer loose in appearance. The tarts will only need about 8-10 minutes.

• Lachlan, companion to Duncan and Diane

Quick Tuna Protein Boost

This works perfectly if you have made the previous recipe as it gives you a use for the leftover tuna. Also, switching it up with light flaked salmon is just as satisfying.

Ingredients

Light flaked tuna	3 tbsp
Celery (diced)	¼ cup
Hardboiled eggs	2

Method

Place a pot of water with a teaspoon of salt to boil on high heat. When the water comes to a boil gently drop the whole, raw eggs in and cook for 11 minutes. Immediately run under cold water until completely cooled. Peel the cooled eggs, ensuring there is no shell remaining on them and roughly chop them. Toss with remaining ingredients.

Note: I usually mix this with my dogs' dry food in the morning. If they're eating in the evening, I don't like to give them a lot of protein as they don't digest it as well as they are less active late in the day.

• Teddy, companion to Bruce,
Yoshiko and Amos

Soybeans in Olive Oil, Mint and Parsley

For all you vegans out there, this is a good protein supplement. This may be the easiest recipe ever. So if you are busy and you have a dog that can't have much sodium or natural sugars, or you can't get your hands on a decent protein source, try this. You can buy soybeans, fresh or frozen, and both are a very suitable source of protein.

Ingredients

Soybeans	1 cup
Olive oil	1 ½ tsp
Mint (chopped)	1 tsp
Parsley (chopped)	1 tsp

Method

Using a small mixing bowl, gently toss all ingredients together and serve. Makes one serving.

***

Note: *Don't overdo the oil. Large amounts, even of healthy olive oil, may result in loose bowels.*

• Cooper,
  companion to
  Corey and John

Photo: Emma Braun

Sunflower encrusted chicken strips

with carrot and sour cream purée

Sunflower seeds are extremely nutritious, containing 24 percent protein and a great balance of essential amino acids. Also, they just give a fun crunch. When I make this for my dogs, I usually get my sunflower seeds from a health food store so I know there are no additives or extra sodium.

Ingredients

Skinless boneless chicken breast	1
Sunflower seeds (chopped)	½ cup
Whole wheat flour	1 cup
Eggs (lightly beaten)	2
Carrot (cooked and mashed)	1 cup
Sour cream	1 tbsp
Fresh dill	1 tsp

When serving, I like to make a layer of carrot purée on the bottom of the bowl and chop up the chicken into bite-sized pieces. Makes two servings for a small dog and one serving for a medium to large dog.

Note: *Carrots can be substituted with sweet potato just as easily.*

Method

Pre-heat oven to 350°F. Cut chicken breast into 6 strips and set in fridge. Once the seeds are chopped up, add ½ cup of whole wheat flour and pour onto a plate. Lightly beat the eggs in a small bowl and pour the remainder of the wheat flour onto a separate plate. Now we have a breading station. Align all ingredients in a line starting with your chicken, then your flour, then the beaten egg, next the seeds and flour mix, and lastly a lined baking tray. Using two hands, one for dry and one for wet, dredge the strips one at a time in the flour. Then add in the egg wash and lastly in the seed and flour mixture. Once this is complete, place chicken strips in the oven for 15- 20 minutes or until they reach 160°F. Let cool slightly before serving.

For the purée, simply mix the sour cream and fresh dill into the cooked and mashed carrots.

• Winnie, companion
  to Andrea, and Owen

White fish crusted with ground brown rice
with herbed green beans

This recipe is very suitable if you are watching your dog's fat intake. Most fish contains very healthy fatty acids. And the brown rice adds a nice source of fiber.

Ingredients

White fish such as pickerel or sole (boneless)	4 oz
Ground brown rice (available pre-ground at health food stores)	1 cup
All purpose flour	1 cup
Eggs	2
Green beans (fresh)	½ cup
Parsley	1 tsp
Dill	2 tsp

Method

Pre-heat oven to 350°F. Clean any bones out of fish if not already cleaned and set in fridge. Pour ground brown rice onto a plate. Place the lightly beaten egg in a small bowl and the flour on a separate plate. Align all ingredients in a line starting with your fish, then your flour, then the beaten egg, then the ground rice, and lastly a lined baking tray. Using two hands, one for dry and one for wet, dredge the fish one at a time in the flour. Then add in the egg wash and lastly in the ground rice. Once this is complete place fish in oven for 10-15 minutes or until it is golden brown. Let cool slightly before serving.

For the green beans, I usually cut them up small and lightly blanch them for about 1 minute so they are still a little crunchy. Once drained, toss with fresh herbs and serve on top of the fish. I like to serve the beans on top to ensure that my sneaky guys eat their vegetables first. Makes two servings for a small dog and one serving for a medium to large dog.

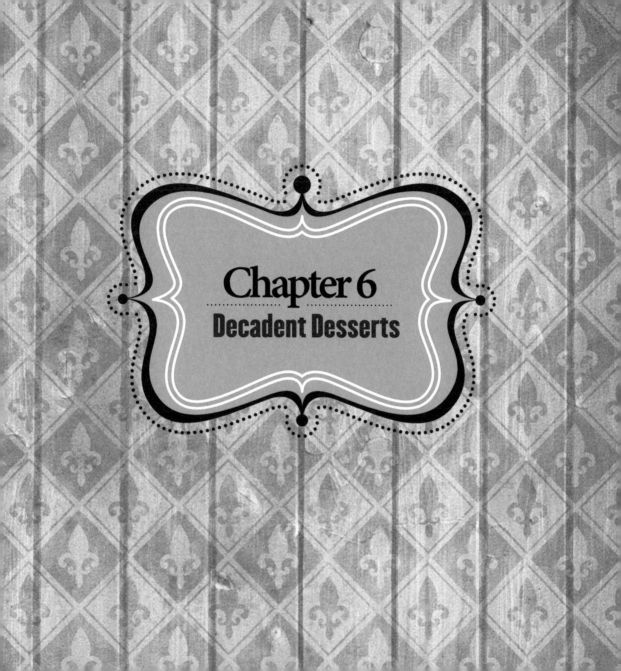

Chapter 6
Decadent Desserts

Who doesn't love dessert? I know I need a pick-me-up every now and again. I remember my first experience with cake. I promptly took the cake my mom had set on my highchair tray and proceeded to shovel it into my face, and I mean shovel. Whatever did not make it into my mouth made it up my nose, and was later sneezed all over an unsuspecting bank teller. Oops! Anyone who knows me even a little will attest to my love of cake. So why not provide my little guys with that same special occasion delight that I have such fond memories of.

　　Of course I know they don't need dessert. They would probably be happy licking the leftovers off my plate. But many dogs do enjoy a sweet taste. These recipes don't call for white sugar or high fructose corn syrup. Instead the sweetness comes from honey, molasses or fresh fruit. How better to celebrate a dog party, the holidays, or doggy play-dates?

Fudge for your Fido

I like to save these for more of a summer treat. I keep them in my freezer and give my guys one when they look like they've lounged in the sun a little too long.

Ingredients

Margarine	1 cup
Molasses	¼ cup
Eggs (lightly beaten)	6
All purpose flour	1 cup
Whole wheat flour	1 cup
Carob powder	½ cup
Baking powder	1 tsp

Method

Cream margarine and molasses together until pale in color. Add eggs one at a time until all is incorporated. Sift in remaining ingredients and mix well until incorporated. Pour mixture into a lined 16x16-inch pan or two 8x8-inch pans. Bake for 20-25 minutes in a 350°F oven or until mixture is set. Cut into bite-sized pieces and freeze until ready to use.

Carob Banana Cake
with honeyed cream cheese frosting, or carob ganache

Surprisingly this is a recipe I use quite often in the restaurant for wedding cakes, as it keeps its moisture really well. I just played around with the original ingredients and made it a little more nutritious.

Ingredients

All purpose flour	1 cup
Whole wheat flour	1 cup
Baking soda	2 tsp
Carob powder	2 tbsp
Honey	¼ cup
Vegetable oil	½ cup
Banana (puréed)	½ cup, about 2
Vinegar	2 tbsp
Water	2 cups

Method

In large bowl combine honey, oil, banana, vinegar, and water. Sift in dry ingredients and whisk until there are no noticeable lumps of flour remaining. Pour into two 10 inch pans lightly greased with cooking spray. Bake for 20-30 minutes at 350°F or until a toothpick comes out clean. Set aside to cool. Cream cheese frosting follows.

• P'nut, companion to
Kathy and Ben

Honeyed Cream Cheese Frosting

Ingredients

Low fat cream cheese	3 cups (about 2 packages)
Honey	2 tbsp
Whole milk	3 tbsp

Method

Pull cream cheese out of refrigerator for a minimum of 20 minutes to soften slightly. In a large bowl cream together cheese and honey. Whisk in milk. If icing is too thick to spread, add another tablespoon of milk.

Putting cake together: You should have two layers of cake baked and cooled. Take cakes out of pan and with a serrated knife trim one layer so that it is flat on top and bottom. Spread half of the frosting on this cake layer. Place other cake layer on top. Spread remaining frosting on top of cake, cut and serve. This will last in the refrigerator for up to a week. Decorate with a few carob chips if you feel like jazzing it up a little.

Or you can try the following frosting for variety:

Carob ganache

Ingredients

Carob chips	1½ cups
Margarine	3 tbsp

Method

Place a pot of water over medium heat until it comes to a simmer. Place chips and margarine in a heat-proof bowl over the hot water, or use a double-boiler, and stir until all is melted and well incorporated. Take off the heat and place plastic wrap directly onto ganache and let it cool to room temperature or until you have a spreadable consistency.

Super Moist, Dense Pumpkin Cake

This is another recipe I use often in the restaurant that I've altered to be more nutritious. At work, I swap out different fruits and vegetables to provide completely different flavours. I think you will enjoy this yourself.

Ingredients

Honey	¼ cup
Eggs	2
Vegetable oil	1 cup plus 1 tbsp
Pumpkin purée (no additives)	4 cups
Apple (shredded)	1 cup
Yogurt	½ cup
All purpose flour	¾ cup
Whole wheat flour	¾ cup
Baking soda	1 tsp

Method

In a large bowl whisk together honey, eggs and oil until pale in color. Add carrot, apple, and yogurt. Mix just until incorporated. Sift in dry ingredients. Stir just to incorporate. Pour batter into 2 greased 10-inch cake pans. Bake for 30-40 min at 350°F or until toothpick comes out clean. Place on a cooling rack until completely cooled. For frosting, use the previous cream cheese frosting recipe adding a tsp of ground cinnamon. To add a chocolate flavour to this recipe just replace yogurt with melted carob chips.

If your dog has diarrhea, pure pumpkin purée will firm up his stool. If your dog is constipated it will help loosen. It's a miracle food!

- ½ tsp for dogs up to 30 pounds
- 1 tsp for dogs 30-60 pounds
- 2tsp-1tbsp for dogs over 60 pounds

• Lucy, companion to
Dennis and Edna

Photo: Emma Braun

Classic Coconut Shortcakes

Again this is a reappearing dessert on my own menu. I have really sensitive teeth and I find these shortcakes easy on them. I figured my dogs would also enjoy the soft texture.

Ingredients

All purpose flour	1 cup
Whole wheat flour	1 cup
Coconut (unsweetened)	¼ cup
Baking powder	1 tbsp
Low fat butter (cut into small pieces and chilled)	½ cup
Egg	1
Whole milk	½ cup
Honey	2 tbsp

Method

In large bowl combine all dry ingredients. Add chilled cubed butter to dry ingredients and mix until small pea-sized pieces form. Place bowl in refrigerator for 15 minutes. While you're waiting for that to chill, in a separate bowl whisk together egg, milk, and honey. Pour this mixture over chilled flour and butter. Mix together using your hands just until it forms a dough. If you find it is a little dry, just add a little more milk. Be careful not to mix too much; over mixing will result in stiff biscuits. Roll out dough on floured surface to ¼ inch thick. Cut into 2-inch square pieces and bake on a lined cookie sheet for 8-10 min at 350°F or until golden brown. Let cool before serving.

This recipe also doubles as a savoury item. Just replace the coconut with grated cheese and add ¼ cup of diced cooked bacon. Makes about 3 dozen small biscuits. Store in an airtight container.

Chapter 7

Home Remedies

Although cooking is the best job I could ask for, it doesn't always rake in the big money. So I've come to rely on alternative methods of relieving my dogs' minor aches and pains as a money saver. This strategy also benefits our environment by not consuming mass-produced products, chemicals, and unnecessary packaging. However, do consult your veterinarian in the event that maladies continue.

Dry cracked paws:

Take one cup of oil, such as coconut, olive or almond, and gently heat together with ½ cup of grated beeswax and gently massage into affected area. Also if you feel like going an extra step, adding a few drops of vitamin E is very beneficial. If your dog has been in the sun for a while and you think he may have burnt his nose, try mixing in 2 tbsp of pure Aloe Vera. It will be very soothing.

Smelly and loose fur:

Living in Canada, my dogs are accustomed to long, very frigid winters. Although they

Inside and out, apple cider vinegar is good for your dog! Start with a tiny amount in your dog's water and very gradually, increase to a tsp a day. Apple cider vinegar is good for arthritis, allergies, itchy skin, correcting pH levels, eliminating tear stains around eyes and fighting fleas!

may have their own reasons to complain, winter causes bigger problems for me. They get fewer baths during these cold months, and as a result, come spring I have two smelly, shedding dogs. So at least once a month I rub them down with a small bit of soda bicarbonate (baking soda). It gets rid of their not-so-fresh aroma and, if you have a small dog like I do, you will avoid the shiver-fest that follows a bath. As for the spring-time drop of loose fur, which I presume you all love as much as I do, I simply use a moistened sponge. All of the loose fur sticks to the sponge and not your pants or bed.

Chewing:

I have watched my two dogs grow up over the years. It has been a delight seeing them develop alongside me. I don't know about your puppies but one of mine ate everything and anything including remote controls, clothes, my leather shoes, and even my floor. So I started using clove oil. It's inexpensive and it has a pungent burning taste that most dogs will be appalled by. My big-gest problem was my guy chewing on my grand-mother's cherrywood end tables. I rubbed some of the oil on the places where he would chew and after his first taste he wasn't back. Other oils such lavender oil are also just as displeasing to their senses, yet not hazardous nor do they harm the furniture finish.

Itch and scratch:

There are many possibilities as to why your dog may be itchy. There could be an allergen present, or they may have naturally dry skin or even ear mites. My guys get very flaky dry skin during

A few drops of lavender

essential oil applied to your dog's tummy can reduce anxiety.

the winter, and I often notice them scratching quite regularly. Soaking them in a cool bath with plain natural oatmeal will sooth their skin. If your dog is scratching his ears, it may be ear mites. One of the tell-tale signs of this is a dark waxy-looking substance in their ears. Using some mineral oil and gently swabbing with a cotton ball will ease the itch temporarily. As it is only temporary, seeing a vet immediately for an antibiotic would be ideal.

Swallowing medication:

My dogs have a little bit of a cat treat-thieving problem, so when I need to get them to take their heart worm pill or any other medication, I turn to the cat treat. Usually hiding your dog's medication in his favorite treat will do the trick. For a more uncooperative dog, rub or gently blow into his nose triggering a licking response. He will have swallowed his pill before he even knows what is going on.

Bleeding nails:

If you are ever cutting your dogs nails and you accidentally cut into the quick and it starts bleeding, don't worry. Placing some cornstarch in a small bowl and dipping your dog's paws in it will stop the bleeding. Most of the time the nail is not that bad, but in rare instances that the bleeding continues consult your vet.

The most important way to prevent bladder problems is water consumption so make sure your dog always has access to fresh water.

• Mocha, companion to Shelly and Scott

CONVERSION CHARTS

Equivalents for Dry Ingredients by Weight

(To convert ounces to grams, multiply the number of ounces by 30.)

1 oz=	1/16 lb=	30 g
4 oz=	¼ lb=	120 g
8 oz=	½ lb=	240 g
12 oz=	¾ lb=	360 g
16 oz=	1 lb=	480 g

Equivalents for Liquid Ingredients by Volume

¼ tsp=			1 ml
½ tsp=			2 ml
1 tsp=			5 ml
3 tsp=	1 tbsp=	½ fl oz=	15 ml
2 tbsp=	⅛ cup=	1 fl oz=	30 ml
4 tbsp=	¼ cup=	2 fl oz=	60 ml
5¾ tbsp=	⅓ cup=	3 fl oz=	80 ml
8 tbsp=	½ cup=	4 fl oz=	120 ml
12 tbsp=	¾ cup=	6 fl oz=	180 ml
16 tbsp=	1 cup=	8 fl oz=	240 ml
1 pt=	2 cups=	16 fl oz=	480 ml
1 qt=	4 cups=	32 fl oz=	960 ml
	33 fl oz=	1000 ml=	

Photo: Natasha Kilfoil

• **Quincy, companion to Lavonne, Des, Natasha and Lauren**

Equivalents for Cooking/Oven Temperatures

	Fahrenheit	Celsius
Freeze water	32	0
Room Temperature	68	20
Boil Water	212	100
Bake	325	160
	350	180
	375	190
	400	200
	425	220
	450	230

• Cash, companion to Suzanne and Branden

• Billie, companion to
Jeanette and Dale

Reading List

Adamson, Eve, Chow Hound: *Wholesome Home Cooking for Your Doggie,* 2009: New York, NY, Sterling Publishing Co., 144 pg

Armstrong, Karen, *Dog Food Recipes Cookbook,* 2010: Scotts Valley, CA, Createspace, 154 pg.

Brown, Steve, *Unlocking the Canine Ancestral Diet,* 2009: Wenatche, WA, Dogwise Publishing, 133 pg.

Fox, Michael, Elisabeth Hodgkins, & Marion Scott, *Not Fit for a Dog*, 2008: Fresno, CA, Linden Publishing, 200 pg.

O' Grady, Patricia, *Woofing it Down: The Quick and Easy Guide to Making Healthy Dog Food at Home,* 2007: Bloomington, IN, Authorhouse, 124 pg.

Olson, Lew, *Raw & Natural Nutrition for Dogs: The Definitive Guide to Home-made Meals,* 2010: Berkeley, CA, North Atlantic Books, 226 pg.

Palika, Liz, *The Ultimate Pet Food Guide: Everything You Wanted to Know About Feeding Your Dog or Cat,* 2008: Jackson, TN, Da Capo Press, 256 pg.

Peterson, Melissa M., *Canine Cuisine,* 2010: Ocala, FL, Atlantic Publishing Co.

Poveromo, Mark, *To Your Dog's Health! Canine Nutrition and Recent Trends Within the Pet Food Industry,* 2010: web, Poor Man's Press, 88 pg.

Pugnetti, Gino, *Simon & Schuster's Guide to Dogs,* 1980: New York, Simon & Schuster, 448 pg.

Roache, M., & Dr. K. L. Rainey, *Complete Dog Food Reference Guide,* 2010: Scotts Valley, CA, Createspace, 828 pg.

Talley, Jessica Disbrow & Eric, *The Organic Dog Biscuit Cookbook from the Bubba Rose Biscuit Company,* 2008: Kennebunkport, ME, Cider Mills Press, 222 pg.

- thedogbowl.com
- thebuzzel.com
- animalwellnessmagazine.com
- animals.howstuffworks.com
- gourmetsleuth.com
- nlm.nih.gov/medlineplus/pethealth.html
- dogandcollar.com
- ca.dir.yahoo.com/Science/Biology/Zoology/Animals__Insects__and_Pets/Pets/Health/

Index